"What Did I Do Wrong?"

An Accessible Guide to Preventing Traumatic Misunderstandings Between You and Your Autistic Loved One

By Jaime A. Heidel – The Articulate Autistic

"What Did I Do Wrong?" - An Accessible Guide to Preventing Traumatic Misunderstandings Between You and Your Autistic Loved One

Table of Contents

Acknowledgments

I'd like to thank each and every one of my readers who have supported, encouraged, and collaborated with me over the past few years; you've been incredible. Without you, this book never would have happened, so each page of it is, first and foremost, dedicated to you.

I'd also like to acknowledge my incredible partner, Kat, who understood me the second she laid eyes on me, and who I never have to explain myself to. I'm so blessed to have you at my side in this strange journey called life.

To Auntie Kate; you're the reason I'm still on this planet, and not a day goes by that I don't know it and appreciate it. When nobody else believed me, understood me, or even wanted me around, you did, and I am forever grateful.

And to my mom, whose brain is so similar to mine—(or is that the other way around)—I wish I could just "feel" your dedication to you because no words will ever adequately express the sentiment that has grown for you in my heart.

To my estranged family, I spent decades explaining myself to you in the most articulate, detailed ways possible, only for that (very neurodivergent) way of expressing myself to be the primary reason you didn't believe me even after I was diagnosed. The irony. After I finally had enough and walked away from the toxicity, I spent some much-needed time collecting myself and every word you discarded, posted both online, and found not only validation and community, but a beautiful way to turn trauma into knowledge and pave an easier path for the next generation of autistics.

"It is easier to build strong children than to repair broken men." - Frederick Douglass.

Sir, I couldn't agree with you more.

Now—let's get started on that, shall we?

Introduction

If you've picked up this book, chances are you either have an autistic person in your life who you don't understand as well as you would like – and it's causing a frustrating amount of miscommunication, or you're an autistic person who wants and needs their neurotypical (non-autistic) loved ones to understand them, so these painful miscommunications don't continue.

Either way, welcome! I'm Jaime A. Heidel, The Articulate Autistic. I'm a late-diagnosed autistic and ADHD woman who specializes in translating autistic communication and behavior for the neurotypical (non-autistic) mind.

I've dedicated my life to helping neurotypical people understand their autistic loved ones because a lifetime of chronic misunderstandings often leads to the development of complex PTSD on the part of the autistic person.

I am one of those autistic people with complex PTSD, and I have dozens if not hundreds of miscommunication horror stories that have done serious and irreparable harm to my mental health.

Thankfully, my love for and gift of writing has never left me, no matter what I've been through, and I can use what I've experienced to help the future generation of autistic people grow up in a world with more understanding and less miscommunication trauma.

Throughout the rest of this book, I'll be talking directly to my neurotypical readers, so buckle up, open your mind, and journey with me on a deep dive into the world of autistic traits, intentions, communication, and behavior like you've never seen it explained before.

You're Unintentionally Traumatizing Your Loved One Every Day

Let's rip the bandage off right away, and expose what's festering underneath, shall we? Allow me to bluntly tell you that you are most likely traumatizing your autistic loved one (at least a little bit) every day. And, unless you're a terrible person, you're not doing it on purpose.

In fact, I'm willing to bet that you may even be afraid to interact with your autistic loved one at times for fear that you may accidentally hurt them! And, as commendable as that is, it's certainly not a sustainable way to live.

You can't spend the rest of your life feeling as though you're walking on eggshells, and your autistic loved one can't spend the rest of their life wondering when the vultures are going to descend*.

* "The Attack of the Vultures" is a term I coined over 10 years ago to describe what it was like to live as an autistic person in a neurotypical world where everything was fine one minute, and someone was yelling at me for offending them the next. I never knew when it was coming, I could not connect my behavior or words to their reaction, and I lived most of my life terrified of others thinking that they just randomly exploded on people for no reason!

So, what is it that's so traumatic about simply being an autistic person in a neurotypical world? Well, aside from sensory overload caused by a heightened sensitivity to lights, sounds, smells, textures, etc., we live in a world where the majority of the people around us (the neurotypical people) speak a completely different social language from us, and these same people, not realizing it, attribute our natural autistic traits, communication style, and behavior to purposeful malice – because when neurotypical people do the same things that we do (for completely different reasons) – or, at the very least, disrespect and rudeness are actually the intent!

That's a very painful thing to discover, by the way. Most of us are bowled over in shock when we finally connect the dots as to why so many people are angry with us all the time!

The Way You View Us vs Who We Really Are

I'll start this part off by saying that autistic people are individuals, first and foremost. We may have a lot in common, but we are not, by any means, exactly alike. Not everything you read in this book will apply to the autistic person in your life. In fact, some things may be contradictory or may not even apply.

This book is a comprehensive guide meant to explain the most common misunderstandings I've come across in my time writing, advocating, and translating for the autistic community. So, take what you need, and leave the rest.

Now that we've gotten that out of the way, let's talk about the core reason miscommunication between the neurotypes can cause so much pain and trauma, and that core reason is the startlingly large chasm of a difference between how you view us versus who we really are.

As a neurotypical person, you view the world through a neurotypical lens. For you, that's "normal". As an autistic person, I view the world through an autistic lens, and for me, *that's* "normal".

Now, autistic people who are placed in behavior modification plans (that I vehemently disagree with) are forced to learn how neurotypical people view the world, socialize, show empathy, make friends, express emotion, move and use their bodies, and communicate with others. These same autistic people, usually children, are then forced to emulate these traits to make the neurotypical people around them more comfortable.

I believe this practice to be barbaric. However, I don't disagree with both autistic and neurotypical people learning each other's social languages. I think there could be great benefit in that. Unfortunately, as it stands, that "learning" only goes one way, and it's forced, causing harm and trauma.

Neurotypical children are never forced to learn autistic traits, communication, and behavior and then punished if they don't comply, and I would never advocate for that. It would be just as wrong, just as traumatic, and just as harmful.

However, if neurotypical people could be taught, with consent and care, about how autistic people view, respond to, and move about in the world, I believe there would be far fewer traumatic misunderstandings – and that's what this guide aims to do.

Each of the things I'll explain in this guide are things commonly viewed by neurotypical people to be rude, uncaring, cruel, or even downright malicious.

Because of the large gap between autistic intention and how the action behind said intention is viewed through a neurotypical lens, autistic people often have great difficulty connecting our behavior to your angry and offended response.

It seems to come out of nowhere; the attack of the vultures.

The Confusing and Traumatic Accusations We Receive Everyday

Those who are unaware of the significant communication differences between autistic and neurotypical people often mistake our everyday actions as any one of the following (or a combination thereof):

- Hiding something
- Having a hidden agenda
- Having an angle
- Trying to get attention
- Trying to be dramatic
- Being ungrateful
- One-upping others
- Being selfish
- Making everything about us
- Being overly picky
- Being controlling
- Being manipulative
- Being aggressive
- Being bored or disinterested
- Being rude
- Angling to steal someone's job
- Trying to steal someone's romantic partner
- Trying to cause conflict or drama
- Not caring about others
- Being cold and calculated
- Disrespecting authority
- Secretly hating everyone
- Playing innocent
- Playing victim
- Feeling sorry for ourselves
- Holding grudges
- Thinking we are better than others
- Being lazy and unmotivated
- Making excuses

Imagine, for one moment, that you've been accused of every single one of these things at least once throughout your life when you had no idea what was going on and no intention of hurting anyone else. Can you even fathom what a life like that would be like?

That's the kind of life so many autistic people are forced to endure because nobody will believe us when we explain that we weren't even *thinking* of doing whatever it was we're being accused of, never mind actually doing it.

That's how we're traumatized every day. Are you unintentionally doing this to your autistic loved one? Keep reading.

How to Use This Book

Since every autistic person is unique, there can be no true definitive guide to your autistic loved one's specific neurology. Therefore, the best way to use this book is as a guide, a blueprint that can help you gain a better understanding of your autistic loved one's way of thinking and communicating, as well as their intentions – a steppingstone to better understanding, if you will.

The best way to truly understand the autistic person in your life is to communicate with them directly in whatever format works best, so they can guide you through their own individual experiences, feelings, thoughts, and ideas.

The best guide to understanding an autistic person lies within the autistic person themselves as there will never be a book out there that describes **them** unless they write it themselves.

So, read, take notes, share these words with them, ask, answer, listen, keep an open mind, and, most important of all, *believe them*.

Autistic Trait: Direct Communication.

Common Misinterpretation(s): Being controlling, manipulative, or aggressive. Trying to cause conflict or drama. Disrespecting authority.

What's Really Happening:

Autistic people are usually pretty direct communicators. We say what we mean, and we mean what we say. Unlike neurotypical speakers, who use a combination of words, tone, body language, and context clues to convey information and feelings, autistic people rely on the literal meaning of the spoken or written word to communicate directly. We also benefit greatly from others communicating in the same way with us; clear, concise, literal, and to the point.

With the autistic person in your life, the words they are speaking mean exactly what they intend to convey. Avoid trying to decipher meaning that isn't there and then responding to what you *believe* is the intended meaning. This is very confusing for autistic people and can cause an immediate and jarring disconnect in communication.

Furthermore, if your autistic loved one's words are saying one thing, but their facial expression, body language, tone of voice, etc., are appearing to "say" another, ***pay attention to and respond to only the literal words***. Oftentimes, autistic people are unaware of what our bodies, faces, and vocal tone are doing, and when others respond to those instead of our words, it creates unnecessary confusion and distress.

An autistic person who is speaking directly, with literal meaning, has no intention of being controlling, manipulative, or aggressive, and they are not trying to cause drama or disrespect your authority or knowledge on a subject. This is just our social language. This is how we speak to each other, as well, and there is usually no misunderstanding of this direct and literal communication – in fact, it's actually how we avoid misunderstandings!

Autistic Trait: Forgetting important events.

Common Misinterpretation(s): Being selfish, not caring about others, and/or secretly hating someone.

What's Really Happening:

While many autistic people have a fantastic memory, there are also many of us who really struggle. As an autistic/ADHD person, a combination of poor working memory, poor short-term memory, and poor time awareness cause me to instantly forget anything that is not within my immediate field of awareness. Like many AuDHD (autistic and ADHD combined) folks, I struggle mightily with object permanence. This means anything that is out of sight is also out of mind.

I also struggle with something known as "time blindness". Unlike many of my neurotypical counterparts, I cannot accurately gauge how long it's been since I've last seen or interacted with someone, how long I've known a person, or how long I've worked on a project – unless I make constant use of clocks, calendars, and reminder apps.

Birthdays, holidays, anniversaries, and other events that the large majority of society thinks about and celebrates regularly are things I don't think about or celebrate. I don't even make a fuss about my own birthday, and my partner and I (both autistic/ADHD) acknowledge anniversaries when we remember to, but we don't even think to make a big celebration of them.

If you've noticed the autistic person in your life forgets to acknowledge events that are important and special to you, this doesn't mean they are being selfish, uncaring, or that they're holding some secret grudge against you. They most likely have completely forgotten about it! There's no hidden social meaning behind it; it's just down to a neurological difference.

Autistic Trait: Lack of reciprocity.

Common Misinterpretation(s): Being selfish, being manipulative, not caring about others, making everything about us, secretly hating someone, holding grudges.

What's Really Happening:

Your autistic loved one actually doesn't lack reciprocity. It's that they're showing it in a different way than what you've come to expect as a neurotypical person. See, when autistic people communicate with one another, we don't wait to be asked how we are doing, we just tell the other person, and they do the same with us!

The literal interpretation of words is another reason why you may feel your autistic loved one doesn't show reciprocity. For example, let's say you send the autistic person in your life a text message: *"Hope everything is going well!"* and the autistic person responds with: *"Everything is fine, thanks!"* To the autistic person, a quick, literal text exchange happened, and now it's over. To the neurotypical person, however, the response may feel like a slight because they believe the autistic person purposefully ignored their social bid.

Here's the thing, to the autistic brain, **there *was* no social bid**! The words in the text were received and interpreted literally! If the neurotypical person then responds to the autistic person's literal response to the text with, *"You're so selfish! Don't you care how I'm doing?"* the autistic person won't have any idea where this sudden anger or hurt came from, and it will cause unnecessary distress.

Poor memory is another contributing factor to an apparent lack of reciprocity. You may have previously told them about an important upcoming event in your life (such as surgery, a move, a wedding, etc.), but they don't follow up with you because the information is simply no longer in their brain!

Autistic Trait: Dropping, breaking, or running into things.

Common Misinterpretation(s): Trying to get attention, trying to be dramatic, being aggressive, not caring about others or their property, trying to cause conflict or drama, secretly hating others, and holding grudges.

What's Really Happening:

Many autistic people struggle with their proprioception, meaning they have difficulty sensing where their bodies end and where other objects begin. Many also have dyspraxia, which causes difficulties in planning and processing motor tasks.

These factors can lead to an unsteady or atypical gait, a tendency to drop, break, or run into objects, a tendency to run into other people, and a lack of overall coordination.

These coordination challenges can also significantly interfere with tasks that require gross and fine motor skills such as playing sports, tying shoes, operating machinery, opening jars, and assembling puzzles, toys, or furniture.

Many autistic people, myself included, have to manually compensate for these challenges every time we move through a space, so we don't drop or break anything. This can take a lot of mental effort, and if we've been doing it for long enough, we may not even realize we're doing it and just how on edge we are until we are finally able to sit down again!

If the autistic person in your life has these struggles, keep breakable objects of monetary and sentimental value safely tucked away.

Autistic Trait: Kind, helpful behavior.

Common Misinterpretation(s): Having a hidden agenda, having an angle, trying to get attention, being manipulative, trying to steal someone's job, trying to steal someone's romantic partner, and thinking we are better than others.

What's Really Happening:

When I was a child, teen, and young adult, I was selflessly kind and helpful – from a neurotypical point of view, off-puttingly so. Due to my complex PTSD, my brain has trauma-blocked many details in my life, so I don't actually remember what I did specifically that was so bothersome to people, but I do remember their responses: *"What is your angle?" "People aren't kind for no reason!" "What do you want?" "Why are you always trying to 'help'? People don't want your help!"*

None of it ever made sense to me. I was just doing what came naturally to me; being helpful, kind, loving, and genuine. It never occurred to me to even want something in return from these people. I wasn't trying to manipulate them, coerce them, or get them to "owe" me favors – I didn't even know that was something you could do! I never had expectations from anyone. I was just being me.

The neurotypical norm for friendships appears to be transactional and based on a mutually beneficial model. You do something for me, I do something for you. You give a compliment; I pay you one in return. You give me a gift; I give you one in return.

By contrast, autistic friendships appear to be more free-flowing and collaborative in nature with little importance placed on how useful others are or "keeping score" by paying favors, compliments, and gifts "back".

Autistic Trait: Spontaneous gift-giving.

Common Misinterpretation(s): Having a hidden agenda, having an angle, trying to get attention, being manipulative, trying to steal someone's job, trying to steal someone's romantic partner, and thinking we are better than others.

What's Really Happening:

This one is very similar to Kind, Helpful Behavior. Spontaneous gift-giving to show platonic affection is a more common autistic "love language" than I previously realized until I asked other autistic people about it on my Instagram page. It even has an anecdotal name! Penguin pebbling!

If you're unfamiliar, if a penguin likes another penguin, they give it a shiny rock. Crows do something similar. If they like and begin to feel comfortable with a human being, they'll bring shiny objects to show their appreciation.

This is the kind of thing I used to do to show affection, as well. If I liked someone (usually in a platonic way), I would draw something, write something, or give them a little trinket out of the blue. It wasn't their birthday or a holiday, and I wasn't necessarily close with them, but, in my defense, I used to believe anyone who wasn't actively bullying me was my friend – (insert sheepish look here).

Awkward as it may have been, my gift-giving wasn't just seen as "cringe", people truly believed that I was "angling" for something, trying to curry favor, being manipulative, and even love-bombing. Since that wasn't even close to my intention, these accusations didn't make any sense to me and were simply distressing. Granted, I did stop, but I didn't understand for a very long time what it was I had done wrong.

The same may be true for the autistic person in your life.

Autistic Trait: Asking questions.

Common Misinterpretation(s): Being manipulative, being aggressive, trying to cause conflict or drama, disrespecting authority, and/or thinking we are better than others.

What's Really Happening:

It is very common for autistic people to be bottom-up thinkers instead of top-down thinkers like those in the neurotypical majority. Where neurotypical people see the big picture first and the details second, autistic people are the opposite – we need all the details first before we can see and understand the big picture.

Because details are critical to our understanding, many of us will ask lots of follow-up questions when learning new information or listening to someone tell a story about something that happened to them. The more details we have, the more complete the whole picture is in our minds.

When these questions go unanswered, however, many of us struggle to carry out the instructions or fully relate to and understand the personal story being shared because the picture is not complete; it's missing large chunks where important data should be.

Unlike our neurotypical counterparts, most autistic people only ask questions to get answers. Personally, I had no idea that questions also had an underhanded purpose until I was well into adulthood, so it never made sense to me when others continually responded to my genuine inquiries with accusations that I was, "questioning intelligence", "talking back", or "challenging authority".

I don't think that way. When I ask a question, I'm like a detective looking for clues, gathering each clue (answer) and using it as a building block to create a complete picture.

Autistic Trait: Not picking up on subtle social cues

(facial expressions, tone of voice, body language, the silent treatment, making loud noises, frequent sighing, etc.)

Common Misinterpretation(s): Selfishness, being manipulative, trying to cause conflict or drama, and/or secretly hating someone.

What's Really Happening:

When neurotypical people communicate with each other, they use a combination of words, facial expressions, tone of voice, body language, and more to convey their meaning. Neurotypical communication is layered with subtext and context clues that autistic people often don't pick up – often to our emotional detriment and your hurt feelings.

Those who are unfamiliar with how literal the autistic brain is may feel as though they are being ignored or purposefully "messed with" when they give their autistic loved one a 'certain look', pointedly refuse to speak to them, make loud noises like slamming cabinets to indicate frustration, or sigh frequently in an attempt to get them to ask what's wrong – yet their autistic loved one responds to none of it!

The autistic person in your life is not being rude by not responding to these social cues, *they cannot read these social cues!* For many of us, there's no difference between your usual non-verbal communication and your frustrated, irritated, sad, anxious, etc., non-verbal communication. Also, frequent sighing is common in many autistic people and actually doesn't have a social meaning (it's usually a combination of chronic air hunger and forgetting to breathe), so we often don't interpret it as a social cue when others do it.

If you want the autistic person in your life to understand what you need, **tell them explicitly**. When you hint at things instead of saying them outright, you're speaking a foreign and unreadable language.

Autistic Trait: Not picking up or talking long on the phone.

Common Misinterpretation(s): Being selfish, not caring about others, being lazy and unmotivated, and making excuses.

What's Really Happening:

Many autistic people dread talking on the phone for multiple reasons including, being startled by the sound of the phone ringing, struggles with auditory processing, not feeling comfortable with or knowing how to perform "small talk", having difficulty keeping track of the conversation due to poor memory and/or attention struggles, anxiety about routine disruption, pressure to mask tone of voice to avoid seeming uninterested or angry, and social exhaustion.

As a neurotypical person, it may be difficult for you to conceive of all the challenges talking on the phone can present for your autistic loved one because you've never experienced them, or if you have, you're only experienced them very mildly.

To read that a "simple phone call" can cause so much difficulty may seem almost ridiculous to you, but it's important to also remember that it's this mentality that causes so many of us autistic folks to be unable to find the support we need. The first and most important step to providing accommodations for autistic people is to wholeheartedly and emphatically believe in our need for them.

If your autistic loved one avoids phone conversations, try alternative forms of communication such as text, email, or face-to-face video calls.

Furthermore, scheduling phone calls, letting the autistic person set a time limit on the call, and agreeing upon at least one topic of conversation before the call begins are other helpful ways to alleviate some of the anxiety and uncertainty commonly associated with this type of social interaction.

Autistic Trait: "Overdoing" school and work projects.

Common Misinterpretation(s): Having a hidden agenda, having an angle, one-upping others, trying to get attention, angling to steal someone's job, and thinking we are better than others.

What's Really Happening:

When I was a junior or senior in high school, our Home Economics teacher gave us an assignment to "babysit" a 'flour sack child' to get us familiar with the responsibilities of parenting. While most of the students carried their flour sack around on day one, they quickly lost interest and stuffed them in their lockers for the remainder of the assignment, flubbing their answers on the form we were supposed to fill out to track the imaginary day-to-day goings-on in the baby's life.

Not this autistic student! I put the sack of flour inside the outfit of an actual baby doll from my childhood and carried it around with me all week, filling out the paperwork, setting my alarm to wake up in the night, and even getting a real "babysitter" (my best friend at the time) to watch the kid while I was out one night.

After the assignment was over, the teacher took me aside and asked me why I had been so thorough. She told me I didn't have to do all that. My brain about slid out of my skull from confusion, and my heart sank. *"How could doing the right thing be wrong?"* I thought miserably.

If the autistic person in your life appears to do excessive amounts of work, it's not an attempt to one-up or kiss up to anyone. It's a combination of taking instructions literally, all-or-nothing thinking, seeing all aspects of a task as equally important, and having a strong work ethic.

As usual, there's no hidden social agenda. This is just how our brains work.

Autistic Trait: Facial expressions that don't match words and/or current social situation.

Common Misinterpretation(s): Hiding something, being controlling, manipulative, or aggressive, trying to cause drama or conflict, disrespecting authority, secretly hating someone, holding grudges, and thinking we are better than others.

What's Really Happening:

"My brain doesn't tell my face what I'm feeling."

This description is the best way I can think of to explain why my facial expression hardly ever matches what I'm feeling (unless I make a conscious effort to force my facial muscles into the "appropriate" position – which is called 'masking', and it's exhausting, not to mention, harmful to my mental health).

Myself and so many other autistic people have unintentionally caused social upheaval for simply existing in the world with a relaxed face that reads, to neurotypical eyes, as "angry", "sad", "snobby", or "bored".

This is what's known as a 'flat affect'. It's not that autistic people don't have emotions, those emotions just don't seem to reflect on the face.

People have become instantly angry upon meeting me because I appear "unresponsive" to their words. The emotional change in them is so quick and unexpected that, before I knew what was triggering it, I thought nearly everybody just had random emotional outbursts for no reason!

If your autistic loved one tells you they feel a certain way, but their face appears to 'say' something else, believe their words. Insisting that your interpretation of their emotional state is correct, but **their actual feelings** are not can cause anxiety, a distorted sense of self, and an inability to trust one's own intuition.

Autistic Trait: Tones of voice that don't match words and/or current social situation.

Common Misinterpretation(s): Hiding something, being controlling, manipulative, or aggressive, trying to cause drama or conflict, disrespecting authority, secretly hating someone, holding grudges, and thinking we are better than others.

What's Really Happening:

The 'flat affect' that occurs with autistic facial expressions (or lack thereof) often also extends to many autistic people speaking in a monotone. Personally, I have to force inflection into my voice when I speak to others just as I have to manually move my facial muscles into the corresponding facial expression to convey emotion in a way that the neurotypical majority will understand.

In addition to speaking in a monotone (which still happens when I'm far too exhausted to continue masking it), I've also been told I have a rude or sarcastic tone in my voice when I have no intention of it.

Also, since I take what's said to me literally (unless I've had prior experience with a phrase that has multiple meanings), I only just learned this year that when someone says you have a "tone" to your voice, they don't just mean actual vocal tone, they mean your entire vibe, energy, or aura.

So, if you have told your autistic loved one that they need to change their tone, they may have then changed the pitch of their voice and ended up sounding unintentionally sarcastic when trying to do exactly what you asked. If you reacted with anger when they did this, they probably still don't know what they did wrong.

Just like with facial expressions, believe and respond to the actual words, not the tone.

Autistic Trait: Not recognizing your (or their) car in a parking lot.

Common Misinterpretation(s): Trying to get attention, being manipulative, trying to cause conflict or drama, playing innocent, being lazy and unmotivated, and/or making excuses.

What's Really Happening:

This might seem like an oddly specific misunderstanding to include, but it's happened to me, and it was distinctive enough that I wanted to mention it. A little over 10 years ago, I was in my 30s, and I was spending time with a family member who I am now estranged from. They were driving me around since I was in an unfamiliar area, and they dropped me off at a store while they waited in the car.

I got what I needed, came out to the parking lot, and I froze in terror. I suddenly realized I had no idea what color, make, or model of car I had come in! I started looking around frantically, knowing that this family member, who has never believed I'm autistic, was probably thinking I was doing something strange to get attention. By some miracle, I was able to spot the family member in the car, and I walked toward it.

When I told them I couldn't find the car because I didn't remember what car I had come in, they predictably laughed at me. When I asked them why they didn't beep the horn when they saw me struggling, they just shook their head in a typical mixture of disbelief and annoyance I had become accustomed to throughout my life, and it quickly escalated into a bit of a fight until I changed the subject.

If your autistic loved one doesn't know what the family car looks like, believe them. It may have never crossed their mind to pay attention to it. Make accommodations by putting a distinctive decal on the vehicle and help them immediately if they appear lost. This may also happen with their own car, so a distinctive decal and taking a photo of the car and where it's located in relation to other objects before walking away can help.

Autistic Trait: Not recognizing people out of context or when they change their appearance.

Common Misinterpretation(s): Trying to be dramatic, trying to get attention, secretly hating someone, being manipulative, not caring about others, playing innocent, and/or thinking we are better than others.

What's Really Happening:

Many autistic people have prosopagnosia or face blindness. This means that even the faces of familiar people can become unrecognizable when seen out of context, after an extended period of time, and/or when the person changes their appearance.

When I was a child, I would often introduce myself to people at extended family get-togethers (because that's what I'd been instructed to do in order to "be polite"), but it would turn out, more often than not, that I was actually re-introducing myself to people I didn't recognize. (I was accused of pretending, of course.)

I've had trouble recognizing familiar faces all my life. I may see someone and have a feeling of vague recognition, but my brain can't quite make the connection to where I know them from. When someone drastically changes their hair or grows or removes a beard, they become a virtual stranger to me until they speak (I'm better at recognizing voices). I once didn't even recognize my own mother at a Walmart because I wasn't expecting her to be there. I actually needed her to speak before I realized who she was.

This even makes watching movies difficult for me because when two main characters look similar, I have a hard time following the plot. If the autistic person in your life doesn't recognize others, face blindness is likely why.

Accommodate them with verbal reminders and provide reassurance. Not being able to recognize people is unsettling enough without being shamed or disbelieved over it.

Autistic Trait: Not laughing at (or even crying at) "funny" videos, TV, or movies.

Common Misinterpretation(s): Trying to get attention, trying to be dramatic, being manipulative, being cold, having no sense of humor, and/or thinking we are better than others (or we are "above it all").

What's Really Happening:

The kind of humor that you, as a neurotypical person, may greatly enjoy may be the same type of humor that the autistic person in your life not only doesn't find funny but may find distressing and sad.

Videos that depict pranks, teasing, not picking up on social cues and therefore embarrassing themselves, "falling" for an elaborate scheme, and jump scares on unsuspecting citizens just going about their day are all things so many of us autistic folks have to experience every day, with the laughter being at *our* expense!

Humor like this is often not funny to us because it's a reminder of how dangerous it can be to be trusting and literal in a world full of people who find exploiting these traits to be entertaining.

Furthermore, many autistic people are hyperempathetic, meaning we can feel the physical effects of the emotional turmoil the person is going through in the video. Moreover, many autistic folks also experience profound second-hand embarrassment, so the incident affects us the same as if we were the one going through it!

This isn't to say that autistic people have no sense of humor, we just differ in what we find funny compared to our neurotypical counterparts, and that difference should be respected and not taken as a personal offense.

Autistic Trait: Becoming deeply distressed when interrupted.

Common Misinterpretation(s): Trying to be dramatic, being selfish, making everything about us, being overly picky, controlling, and manipulative, being aggressive, trying to cause drama or conflict, and/or disrespecting authority.

What's Really Happening:

When a neurotypical person is interrupted during a focused task, they seem to be able to tend to the interruption and return to the original task as though nothing happened. It may be annoying in the moment, but their brains seem to switch gears easily and without too much upset.

This is often not the case with autistic and autistic/ADHD people. When we react strongly to being interrupted, it can appear, at least from an outside perspective, that we're incredibly self-focused and the only thing that matters is what we need and want – but this is not about selfishness. This is about a difference in how our brains function and what our brains need.

I explain to people that when I'm in hyperfocus, it's like tendrils of thought are winding upward into individual thought bubbles that are all interconnected in the space above my head. It takes a long time for those tendrils to unfurl and connect exactly the way I need them to in order to accomplish my task. When I'm done, the tendrils slowly curl back in, and I'm able to stop working on the task.

However, when I'm interrupted, it's like someone has come along and cut one of the bubbles of thought off the tendril, and all of them snap back into my head with a jarring shock, and my fight-or-flight gets triggered. It feels kind of like being startled awake by an air horn!

Your autistic loved one may need time and warning between tasks just like I do.

Autistic Trait: Offering solutions instead of support in relationships.

Common Misinterpretation(s): One-upping others, being controlling, being manipulative, and/or thinking we are better than others.

What's Really Happening:

You've heard the term "fair weather friend"? I call myself a "foul weather friend" because I tend to walk in after everyone else has walked out. I may have no idea how to relate to you in everyday life situations, I may never remember to call or text, and I probably won't hang out with you on weekends, but when your life falls apart, I'm pretty good in a crisis.

Like many things about being autistic living in a neurotypical world with predominantly neurotypical social norms, I didn't realize that when I offered practical solutions to people when they came to me to vent, not only was I not helping them, *I was actually offending them*!

People would say, *"You're not listening to me!"* I didn't understand. Of course, I was listening. I heard the words you spoke; I thought about what you said, my analytical mind came up with a bunch of solutions to your problem, and I shared those solutions with you. Your problem is now fixed! Isn't that what you wanted? Apparently not.

When I discovered that neurotypical people actually preferred others to just listen without offering any solutions, my brain about short-circuited. And when I found out that it was sympathetic 'listening noises' and the occasional, *"that's heavy"* or *"that's rough"* that made neurotypical people feel heard and supported, I couldn't believe that was real, and I remained in denial for a long time, afraid to try it. After all, it seemed like such an ineffectual and insincere way to be there for someone who was suffering – but then, it worked!

For your autistic loved one, offering solutions may be how they show love, as well. If you want them to just listen to you vent, explicitly say so.

Autistic Trait: Becoming deeply distressed over card games and board games.

Common Misinterpretation(s): Trying to get attention, trying to be dramatic, being aggressive, playing innocent, and/or being lazy and unmotivated.

What's Really Happening:

Some autistic people excel at card games and board games, but I am definitely not one of them, and this may also be true for your autistic loved one. If so, I'd like to explain what may be happening for them.

Several years ago, I was spending time with some now-estranged family members, and they were all playing a card game. I do not understand them, and I was incredibly anxious to try, but they encouraged me to play, and – since I was in my masking renaissance – I reluctantly did. Everything was going fine because a friend of the family was helping me with each step each time it was my turn until another family member coldly told this person to stop, and I couldn't continue playing.

Since I have both a poor working and short-term memory, I could not hold the rules of the game in my head long enough to keep going on my own, so I had to stop. Another reason I struggle with card and board games is that the competitiveness of other people really makes me uncomfortable. Some people play as though their lives depend on it, and this makes them play with an emotional edge that genuinely makes me feel unsafe.

Card and board games can also be a trauma trigger for me because when I was a child, my confusion and tears over them was seen as "purposefully causing drama over something that was supposed to be fun".

They may be a popular pastime, but if card and board games are a trigger, just pass.

Autistic Trait: Becoming deeply distressed and/or avoiding learning new skills.

Common Misinterpretation(s): Being controlling, being manipulative, being aggressive, disrespecting authority, being lazy and unmotivated, and/or making excuses.

What's Really Happening:

If the autistic person in your life becomes distressed at the prospect of learning new skills, or they simply refuse to do it, it can be misinterpreted as being controlling, manipulative, disrespectful, lazy, or another personal failing, but none of these are usually the case. In fact, these types of reactions are often down to anxiety based on how others may have treated them in the past due to underlying learning challenges.

This is very similar to the distress over card and board games section above. For many autistic people, especially those who were late diagnosed, there is a lot of trauma around learning simply because many of us were taught in schools that either didn't recognize or didn't believe in our struggles. We were taught the same way as the neurotypical kids around us, and we were shamed over and over again when we failed to live up to those expectations.

Sharing your knowledge and wisdom with someone can be a great way to bond, but when it comes to your autistic loved one, these things may be met with resistance, distress, and even anger because they may feel there is an expectation or condition attached to these bits of information, and if they cannot understand or absorb them the way you're teaching or explaining them, and if you react negatively to their need to ask follow-up questions, the experience will not be a pleasant one for either of you.

An autistic person who doesn't want to learn a skill or life lesson from you isn't showing disrespect, they're trying to protect themselves.

Autistic Trait: Behaving in a way neurotypical people interpret as "suspicious" or "guilty".

Common Misinterpretation(s): Hiding something, having an angle, being manipulative, being cold and calculated, disrespecting authority, playing innocent, playing victim, and/or making excuses.

What's Really Happening:

Natural autistic traits look like neurotypical signs of lying. Read that again. *Natural autistic traits look like neurotypical signs of lying.* It is very, very important for anyone who interacts with autistic people on even a semi-regular basis to know this, understand this, and commit it to memory.

Autistic people may avoid eye contact, dart their eyes around, fidget, sigh too much, swallow too much or too deeply, wring their hands, startle easily, avoid touch, go situationally mute due to the shock of what they're being accused of, stutter, stammer, try to explain, become emotional when not believed (it is a HUGE trauma trigger for many of us), and give what is considered "too much detail" when retelling events.

All of these are natural autistic traits, not signs of guilt. Some of us, including myself, have complex PTSD from a lifetime of being accused of things we don't understand and never intended, and when we *do* try to explain ourselves using logic, because that's how we communicate, it escalates the situation even more.

The more we explain, the more emotional we get, the more we beg and plead to be heard, the more we unintentionally provoke disbelief, anger, rage, and even abuse until the misunderstanding spirals out of control.

The next time you feel like the autistic person in your life has done something out of malice, remember what you know about them as a person and avoid responding with a knee-jerk reaction to a betrayal that never happened.

Autistic Trait: Immediately responding with questions when they have unintentionally hurt your feelings.

Common Misinterpretation(s): Making everything about us, being controlling, being manipulative, not caring about others, being cold and calculated, playing innocent, playing victim, feeling sorry for ourselves, and/or making excuses.

What's Really Happening:

"What did I do wrong?"

Once I realize I've upset someone, I want to immediately know what I've done, how the other person interpreted what I did, why what I did was considered wrong, and what I can do to avoid doing it in the future. I do this because I'm genuinely startled and confused as to why you're upset, so I want to collect as much information as possible to one, reassure you I had no bad intentions, and two, do whatever I can to avoid doing it again.

If I ask what I did wrong, there is a part of me that's trying to protect myself, of course. After all, for a very long time, it appeared to me as though others just erupted with emotion at me out of nowhere for no reason, so part of that is a trauma response.

I may look at the person who is upset with fear and even suspicion at first because I need to know if I have to get out of the situation immediately for my safety. However, after my fight-or-flight calms down, I want to know so I don't cause unintentional harm again. This is why I ask. When I'm given details about what happened, I can then file those details away for the future, so I don't repeat the offense. This is an attempt to repair a rupture using my logical and analytical mind.

Unfortunately, it's been very rare that this critical query has been answered, which has left me committing the same offense for decades afterward.

Autistic Trait: Overexplaining.

Common Misinterpretation(s): One-upping others, trying to cause conflict or drama, being cold and calculated, and/or thinking we are better than others.

What's Really Happening:

As a bottom-up thinker, I need as many details as possible to understand something and form a complete picture in my head. Because I need so many details, I tend to also *give* lots of details when telling a story, giving instructions, or explaining my intentions when they're misunderstood.

Unfortunately, this backfires on me because excessive details in a story or instructions appear to make neurotypical people feel they're being condescended to, and giving too many details about intentions is often interpreted as outright lying as it is seen as "protesting too much". (Never did understand that one.)

Another reason an autistic person may overexplain is because we are expecting to be told verbally when we've given enough detail to be understood, so we can stop explaining, but we don't usually get that. We keep going on expecting to be stopped when the details are sufficient, and the neurotypical person is politely waiting for us to stop speaking (until they get so annoyed, they blow up).

Furthermore, a common trauma autistic people experience is being chronically misunderstood (hence the creation of this book), so we will painstakingly explain every little nuance and detail in response to a misunderstanding to try to clear it up, and, in doing so, we end up "digging a deeper hole" (further cement the belief we are "lying").

If the autistic person in your life overexplains, they may be giving you what they think you need (in the case of instructions), or they may be panicking (in the case of a misunderstanding).

Autistic Trait: Not responding to flirting or bids for romantic attention.

Common Misinterpretation(s): Being controlling or manipulative, not caring about others, and/or being cold and calculated.

What's Really Happening:

If you're in a romantic relationship with an autistic person, you may think they're losing interest in you when they don't respond to your flirting or bids for romantic attention. In response to what you perceive to be a purposeful slight, you may try to show your feelings through changes in your facial expressions, tone of voice, or body language.

You may also do things such as being more curt in your responses to them, leaving them on read when they text, avoiding scheduling dates, and the like, so they "get the hint" that you're upset with them. After weeks, months, or even years of them "ignoring" your hints, you may end the relationship, only to be completely gobsmacked when they react with shock, hurt, confusion, and pain.

You thought they didn't care at all, and now this? Are they trying to manipulate you?

No. No, not at all. They weren't reading your social cues because their brain is not wired to understand subtle communication. So, they didn't *know* you were flirting with them, they didn't *know* you were upset with them or that you felt slighted, and they only responded when you broke up with them because *it's the only time you've been literal and direct!*

When you're in a romantic relationship with an autistic person, you have to be direct. Even attempts to flirt that you believe are incredibly obvious may not be to your autistic partner. Tell them exactly what you're thinking, what you want, and what you need. Don't only be direct when you're ready to walk away, be direct now.

Autistic Trait: Seems to flirt with you but is shocked when you flirt back.

Common Misinterpretation(s): Being manipulative, trying to start drama, and/or trying to steal someone's romantic partner.

What's Really Happening:

I want to start out by saying that nobody, regardless of gender or neurotype, should ever be subjected to unwanted sexual advances or contact. It doesn't matter if you believe (or actually have been) flirting with each other for a while, if the person tells you they're uninterested, they're uninterested, and that should always be respected.

That said, there are some autistic traits that may be mistaken for neurotypical flirting.

For example, needing to wear tight-fitting clothes for proprioceptive input can be seen as showing off their body, being unaware of how physically close they are to someone else, and/or making intense eye contact due to a lifetime of being trained to look at other people's eyes, and being genuinely kind and friendly to everyone equally, regardless of the situation, social hierarchy, or relationship status of those involved.

Other issues that may occur are not picking up on signs of flirting from others (thereby making it appear as though that type of attention is wanted), and/or being unaware of when someone is asking for a date or more because of their use of code phrases such as "go for a coffee", "come in for a night cap", or "Netflix and chill".

Again, if you ask someone out because you think they've been flirting with you, and they respond with shock and disinterest, don't just assume they were messing with you and respond defensively. They may be autistic and communicate in a different way than you're used to.

Listen to their words, believe their words, respect their words, and let it go.

Autistic Trait: Requests help for "easy" tasks.

Common Misinterpretation(s): Having a hidden agenda, having an angle, trying to get attention, trying to be dramatic, being controlling or manipulative, playing innocent, playing victim, being lazy and unmotivated, and/or making excuses.

What's Really Happening:

Several years ago, I made an earnest plea in a Facebook group where you could request help from home maintenance people to have someone come and install a toilet seat for me. I walked away from the computer for a few hours, came back, and saw a bunch of comments scoffing at my request and making fun of me for asking for help with such an "easy" task.

I felt like I'd been punched in the stomach, and I couldn't understand where all the vitriol was coming from. How could people be upset because I was asking for help in an appropriate place to do so? Why would that anger anyone? Oh, how I've asked myself that question so many, many times in my life. Eventually, a kind person did come over and do it, and I never forgot him. He didn't even charge me even though I had fully expected and offered to pay.

Throughout my life, I've been accused of asking for help for what many would consider an "easy" task because I wanted attention from the person I requested help from, I just wanted to be dramatic, I had some secret agenda, I was just lazy, etc. Nope. None of those things were true. I just needed help. If the autistic person in your life asks for help for something you consider easy, don't question them, don't accuse them, don't shame them, help them.

And don't insist on teaching them to do the thing themselves, either. Remember, for some autistic people, learning is trauma and an attempt to teach can be perceived as an immediate threat to their survival due to PTSD.

Autistic Trait: Being suddenly unable to speak (situational mutism).

Common Misinterpretation(s): Hiding something, trying to get attention, trying to be dramatic, being controlling or manipulative, trying to cause conflict or drama, disrespecting authority, and/or playing victim.

What's Really Happening:

"Situational mutism", more commonly (but inaccurately) described as "selective mutism" is not actually selective on the part of the person experiencing it, but on the part of the brain in overwhelming situations.

When a speaking autistic person suddenly stops speaking, it doesn't mean they have chosen to stop doing so for nefarious reasons. Rather, it is something about their current situation that has caused them to *lose* the ability to speak. The brain is shutting down this ability, not the person, so they don't have control over it.

For me, a sudden accusation or someone suddenly yelling at me, especially when they demand answers, can cause me to immediately become unable to speak. My physical inability to answer, and my attempts to do so through stuttering and stammering make me look immediately guilty in the eyes of the neurotypical observer.

What's really happening is my nervous system is going into fight-or-flight as my brain tries to process why I'm being accused of something "out of nowhere". Since my brain doesn't register non-verbal signs of displeasure in others, I often don't know something is wrong until someone screams at me, which causes me to go situationally mute.

Situational mutism can also be caused by anxiety, sensory overload, social exhaustion, and confusion. If the speaking autistic person in your life is suddenly unable to speak, remember that it's not purposeful behavior, and it's not meant as an offense. They literally cannot physically speak.

Autistic Trait: Being very strict and literal about rules.

Common Misinterpretation(s): Having a hidden agenda, having an angle, trying to be dramatic, being picky, controlling, manipulative, or aggressive, trying to cause conflict or drama, disrespecting authority, and/or thinking we are better than others.

What's Really Happening:

Being strict about rules, being rule-bound, and having black-and-white, all-or-nothing thinking are common hallmarks of being autistic. For me, the reason rules are so set in stone (besides my brain just being wired this way), is that I'm a literal thinker, and I also have gotten in trouble for not understanding or following rules in the past (especially social rules that changed based on neurotypical context differentials I couldn't read), so once I fully understood a rule, I held onto it with a vice-like grip as though I would drown if I let go of it.

My response was part being an autistic person who took things literally (while also having a strong sense of justice) and part being frequently traumatized. As I mentioned, learning rules was very difficult for me, so once I did, I not only held fast to them like a safety line, but I also became fearful for others who wouldn't follow them because I thought they would get hurt or punished, too! Furthermore, I couldn't trust people who didn't follow rules. As soon as someone broke a rule, I became immediately suspicious of them, sometimes even fearful. Who could I trust? Did *anyone* say what they meant and mean what they said? Did everyone lie? It was very unsettling.

Your autistic loved one may feel the same way about rules. You may even find them calling YOU out for breaking them, but it's not out of malice. The reason is usually rooted in fear and anxiety, the feeling that nobody is ever telling the whole truth, and that any move they make could get them into trouble where it didn't before (based on ever-changing neurotypical social contexts that remain largely invisible to autistic people).

Autistic Trait: Feeling uncomfortable and distressed by certain well-liked and well-respected people.

Common Misinterpretation(s): Trying to be dramatic, trying to cause conflict or drama, and/or disrespecting authority.

What's Really Happening:

If your autistic loved one avoids a certain person that others seem to like and respect, it usually doesn't mean the autistic person is being purposefully rude. There's something about that person that makes them feel uncomfortable and unsafe – and it may benefit you, as a neurotypical person, to take notice!

Autistic people are often highly sensitive to our environment and the type of energy or vibe others put off. Many of us also have a built-in threat detection system designed by years of being suddenly yelled at, cut off, fired, dumped, or accused of something we had no intention of doing.

Neurotypical people usually rely on a combination of a person's social and professional reputation, charm, and mannerisms to decide whether someone is trustworthy and safe to be around. While autistic folks *may* also use these methods, we tend to rely more heavily on our pattern recognition, gut instincts, and sensory response to the person.

When something doesn't feel right, our bodies respond before our brains do, that fight-or-flight sense kicks in, and we react on instinct without even considering what the social consequences might be. Think if you met a bear in the woods. You know what it is, you wouldn't stop to question its motives or try to have a polite conversation, you'd just get away from it.

If your autistic loved one avoids someone that others flock to, chances are, they're sensing something potentially toxic or dangerous about the person, and their desire to avoid them should be respected.

Autistic Trait: Struggling to open things.

Common Misinterpretation(s): Trying to get attention, trying to be dramatic, being controlling or manipulative, and/or being lazy and unmotivated.

What's Really Happening:

Since I was a child, I've struggled to open things. Bottles, jars, doors (I sometimes find keys challenging), plastic packaging, resealable bags, jewelry clasps, buttons, etc., You name it, I've probably passed it off to someone to open for me at least once.

When I was a kid, I was given grip-strengthening tools, but they didn't do anything to help me. I don't think it was ever about physical strength, per se, but a combination of low muscle tone, hypermobility, dyspraxia, fine and gross motor struggles, and being unable to connect with and engage the "correct" muscle groups during exertion.

Two things make being unable to open things especially tricky for me. One, I'm hyper-independent. I don't like asking for help, but I frequently need it. Two, as a kid, I was accused of pretending not to be able to open things for attention, and, in response, the adults around me just let me struggle no matter how long it went on for, even if the struggle resulted in a meltdown.

I grew up with adults who believed that helping someone who was having a "tantrum" was just "rewarding attention-seeking behavior" and "fostering dependence on others". (Thank goodness for gentle parenting now!)

If the autistic person in your life needs your help to open things, even if it seems like it should be easy, it's not easy for them, and that's why they're asking for help. Please don't judge them, shame them, or question them. Just open the item and, where applicable, provide tools that can help them more easily open things on their own in the future.

Autistic Trait: Staring off "into space" or daydreaming.*

Common Misinterpretation(s): Trying to be dramatic, being selfish, being manipulative, and/or thinking we are better than others.

What's Really Happening:

*Important Medical Note: Absence seizures should always be ruled out before treating staring spells as sensory breaks. Seek the advice of a medical professional before following any advice in this segment.

Barring the presence of absence seizures or any other serious medical condition, staring spells can usually be safely seen and treated as necessary sensory breaks.

Throughout the day, without thinking about it, I'll suddenly stop and stare into space. My eyes and jaw will go soft, and I'll just stare. A few seconds later, I'm back to doing whatever it is I was doing. Many times, I'll even *keep* doing whatever it is I'm doing while I'm taking a sensory break, especially if the activity I'm engaged in is a repetitive physical one.

For me, these sensory breaks are a need. They help me to self-regulate and keep me from becoming overloaded and overwhelmed. I may find myself taking more frequent sensory breaks if I'm tired, overworked, and/or anxious, but, regardless of my physical or mental state, I take them.

When I did this as a child, teachers and family would startle me out of it, snapping their fingers in front of me and yelling at me to pay attention. Adults thought I was rude because I would suddenly "detach" while they were talking to me, but I didn't do it on purpose. It just happened. I'd take a break, and then I'd "return", but I never lost any time, and I didn't become disoriented when it happened.

If your autistic loved one takes sensory breaks, just let them happen unless they are in immediate danger, as stopping them can trigger meltdowns.

Autistic Trait: Reluctance or refusal to apologize.

Common Misinterpretation(s): Hiding something, being selfish, being controlling, manipulative, or aggressive, not caring about others, being cold and calculated, disrespecting authority, playing victim, and/or thinking we are better than others.

What's Really Happening:

Apologizing has always been something that has been very, very, very difficult for me. It's not that I don't care about the other person or repairing the relationship, it's that I cannot apologize to someone if I have no idea what I did to offend them.

In the past, these scenarios have gone like this:

I do or say something (or I don't do or say something), a person is offended, they tell me off, I ask questions about what's going on, I'm thought of as selfish, they tell me they just want me to apologize, I tell them I can't because I don't know what I did, they refuse to explain what I did because they insist I know, they only want the apology, and I can't give it.

As I've mentioned throughout this book, I'm a bottom-up thinker, so I need lots of details to form a clear picture of what happened in my head. I'm also very analytical, literal, and logical. If I cannot understand what I've done that requires an apology, and I apologize anyway, it's insincere, and I'll most likely do the thing again because I don't have the necessary information I need to not repeat the offense.

If the autistic person in your life struggles with apologizing, they may literally not understand what they've done wrong and need more information. Providing that information accommodates this need.

(It's also important to note that there are plenty of autistic people who apologize all the time, even if they've done nothing wrong.)

Autistic Trait: Expressing exuberant, "child-like" joy when happy.

Common Misinterpretation(s): Trying to get attention, trying to be dramatic, and/or one-upping others. Also, simply being immature.

What's Really Happening:

I'm in my 40s, and I still get the happy-flappies and jump up and down and squeal if I see something adorable, or when I get really excited about an accomplishment or an opportunity. Granted, I usually don't do it in public, but it *would* be my first and natural response if those types of responses weren't considered inappropriate in adults.

It's difficult to describe how I feel in relation to how neurotypical people feel only because I truly don't know what joy feels like for them. I guess the best way I can translate it is I seem to feel the same amount of strong feelings as a neurotypical person winning the lottery when I see a cute puppy hopping up and down, ears just flapping away or a baby with big, puffy cheeks staring innocently at the camera.

Ears and cheeks in general have always given me such an incredible serotonin boost, I almost can't handle how joyful I feel. When I was a child, it was a problem because when I saw something with floppy ears or puffy cheeks, off I went chasing it down and grabbing them. Impulse control equaled zero back then. (Don't worry, I don't do that now. lol!)

Former boundary issues aside, I never did any of this stuff for attention, and I don't feel I'm immature for my age. I just feel everything so deeply, no matter the emotion, that it often comes out in physical ways. When I was younger and didn't realize how my exuberant joy was being perceived, the rage and accusations people responded with felt like a punch in the gut. I forever felt like I was being cut off mid-sneeze, and it caused harm.

If your autistic loved one has this trait, their emotional expression is in direct proportion to what they're feeling. None of it is "put on".

Autistic Trait: Not missing you or forgetting you exist.

Common Misinterpretation(s): Being selfish, not caring about others, being cold and calculated, secretly hating everyone, holding grudges, and/or thinking we are better than others.

What's Really Happening:

This one is never particularly easy to write about because no matter how gently I try to explain it, it still makes me look like a bad person. Truth is, I'm OK with that now. People are going to think what they're going to think, and if I can help one autistic person be better understood by those around them, it's absolutely worth it to me!

So, let me give it to you plain: I don't miss people, and I often forget they exist. Does that make me sound like I have no emotional attachment to anybody or anything? Yep. Is that actually true? Nope.

Not missing someone and/or forgetting someone exists is due to a struggle in the *brain*, not the *heart*. It's called poor object permanence and many autistic/ADHD people have this. It's also called "out of sight, out of mind", and it's the same reason food goes bad in my fridge every week. If I don't see it, it's not there, it doesn't exist. When I do see it again, I'm reminded that it's there, and I'm happy about it again. Finding food in the fridge that I didn't know I had but that hasn't gone bad is like finding buried treasure. It's great!

Obviously, people are much more important than food, but my brain doesn't register the difference. (My heart does, but my brain doesn't. Important distinction.) This means when I'm spending time with you, I feel all the warm, fuzzy feelings of affection and care, but when I'm not spending time with you, you blink out of existence. An image of you may pop fleetingly into my head, but it usually doesn't stick long enough for me to reach out. Your autistic loved one may also struggle with poor object permanence.

Autistic Trait: Being distressed by pranks, jokes, and teasing.

Common Misinterpretation(s): Trying to be dramatic, being overly picky, controlling, and manipulative, having no sense of humor, playing innocent, and/or thinking we are better than others.

What's Really Happening:

Consider this for a moment; the way the autistic brain works is so different from the way the neurotypical brain works, we have to have books like this to translate between the two. And many of us who *do* write books, articles, and social media posts explaining ourselves because we've been traumatized from a lifetime of misunderstandings. With me so far?

So, why would someone who lives in a world where people already don't mean what they say, don't say what they mean, and get quickly (and sometimes dangerously) angry, find pranks, jokes, and teasing funny? Many of us feel like we're being pranked our whole lives, even during ordinary, mundane social interactions, so teasing, jokes, and pranks only add yet another layer of confusion.

Since many of us take what is said to us literally, it's not fun when we react to what we believe is your genuine emotion only to hear, *"I was only teasing! Can't you take a joke?"* or *"I can't believe you took me seriously!"* A neurotypical person may think it's great, but an autistic person may curl into a ball and cry and then, to add insult to injury, be called 'dramatic' or 'attention-seeking' for that very genuine and emotionally vulnerable response.

Couple all of this with a heightened sensory system and hypervigilance due to trauma, and these kinds of "games" are anything but fun. That isn't to say all autistic people dislike teasing, jokes, and pranks, but if the autistic person in your life reacts with distress, respect that it's not funny to them, and don't continue doing it. If you do, you're causing psychological harm.

Autistic Trait: Distress about surprise birthday parties (or birthday parties in general).

Common Misinterpretation(s): Trying to be dramatic, being ungrateful, making everything about us, and/or being controlling, manipulative, or aggressive.

What's Really Happening:

For many autistic people, surprises of any kind are a no-no. For one, surprises cause a disruption in routine, and routine provides the safety, structure, stability, and sameness we need to survive in a spontaneous, unpredictable neurotypical world. Furthermore, routine also provides the prompts many of us need to move from one task to the next.

For example, a teen girl may have a routine that goes something like, 'come home', 'wash up', 'have a snack', 'do homework', 'eat dinner', etc. One day, she comes home, and there are people yelling "surprise". She knows it would seem rude to leave the room and go wash up, so she feels stuck between these two activities, with the equation remaining unbalanced.

While she quickly navigates through trying to get her heart to stop pounding, force her face to look happy, mask her tone of voice, frantically search faces to try to recognize the people in the room out of context, try to mitigate the overwhelming sensory overload caused by the music, decorations, talking, and wrapping paper, she also has to cope with a constant thrumming demand in her head screaming, "wash up, wash up, WASH UP" that drowns out all other coherent thoughts.

This is how meltdowns happen, and this is how Aunt Bea gets offended because her niece ran out of the room screaming in response to her moving in for a hug. All of this can be avoided if you ask the autistic person in your life how they feel about birthday parties before throwing one.

Autistic Trait: Appearing to have little or no emotional response to gifts.

Common Misinterpretation(s): Being ungrateful, being selfish, being overly picky, controlling, or manipulative, not caring about others, being cold and calculated, secretly hating others, holding grudges, and/or thinking we are better than others.

What's Really Happening:

I was in my early 30s when a family member told me I didn't have facial expressions. That's the first time in my life I learned that all the emotions I thought that I was clearly expressing on my face **did not register at all** in the eyes of others. Suddenly, so many things in my life made sense. Not only could I not read other people's facial expressions, but they also couldn't read mine!

I had always wondered why people seemed to get angry with me when I opened a gift during the holidays. I'd hear about it later that people had said I was ungrateful, and they were going to stop getting me gifts. Of course, nobody thought to explicitly explain: *"Hey, you don't make any facial expressions when you open a gift, so we think you're a *****"*, so I was, as usual, left confused by how others viewed me.

To make matters worse, I am notorious for forgetting to say, 'thank you'. As a child, I had to be reminded after I opened every gift because I just couldn't remember to say those specific words. I *felt* gratitude, and I *thought* I was emoting that through my face and body, but the words 'thank you' just wouldn't form in my mouth, or I'd say it because I was prompted, and it came out flat and monotone. Another thing that caused problems was that it took me longer to process the gift I received, so I didn't react in the time expected.

The autistic person in your life may be experiencing similar issues, so avoid assuming they're ungrateful due to their response to a gift (or lack thereof).

Autistic Trait: Not making or wanting friends.

Common Misinterpretation(s): Being selfish, secretly hating everyone, and/or thinking we are better than others.

What's Really Happening:

While many autistic people do want friends, but struggle to find people who accept and respect them for who they are, some do not want friends at all. They feel just fine in their own company or in the company of a pet, and/or they receive all the social interaction they need at work, when out shopping, or online. The desire for a friendship connection beyond that just isn't there.

Unfortunately, we live in a society who sees people who do not have friends as "losers" or worse, potentially dangerous based solely on their lack of desire to mix with others.

However, a person who doesn't want friends may have experienced deep trauma when trying to make friends in the past, or, they may have been forced to spend time with neurotypical children at school, and, instead of making friends, they became a favorite target for bullies.

Another reason an autistic person might not want a group of friends is because friendship maintenance is such a big part of keeping neurotypical friends, and since many of us have poor object permanence, we may not reach out or connect in a way that feels meaningful for the neurotypical person. Even friendships with fellow neurodivergent folks can be tricky to navigate as social interaction of any kind can be draining and exhausting.

If your autistic loved one avoids making friends, resist the urge to talk about how wonderful it is to have them or worse, try to force it on them. Not everyone experiences joy when spending time with others. In fact, for some, it's the exact opposite.

Autistic Trait: Breathing differently.

Common Misinterpretation(s): Being bored or disinterested, showing subtle dislike or sarcasm, being dramatic, and/or being creepy.

What's Really Happening:

Atypical breathing, or respiratory dysrhythmia, is quite common in autistic people, which can result in a feeling of "air hunger", or consistently feeling as though one is not getting enough air. This can result in taking frequent deep breaths, sighing deeply, breathing heavily, and gasping. Furthermore, many autistic people also have chronic sinus and gut issues, which can result in mouth breathing, frequent sniffling, and sudden expulsion of air due to a clogged nose and/or acid reflux.

I didn't realize that breathing was used as a subtle means of communication until I was an adult, so when people accused me of being bored or dramatic, or they claimed I was "doing it for attention", I didn't even know what "it" was.

As was so frequent in my childhood, I couldn't connect my behavior to my family's response. They didn't explicitly say, *"Why are you breathing like that?"* or, what would have been even more helpful, *"You're sighing a lot. What does that mean?"* I didn't even *know* people were referring to the way I breathed – or that it was sending some type of social message! So, when someone said, *"Oh, you're just SO bored, aren't you?"* followed by an eyeroll, it seemed to come out of nowhere. Just a random accusation and anger directed at me for what seemed like no reason.

If your autistic loved one breathes differently, they may not even be aware of it. It's most likely not a subtle signal of anything other than the need to fill their lungs. Deep breathing can also be used for emotional regulation, and the brain will often send signals to the body to take deep breaths in times of stress. Since many autistic people are chronically stressed, this starts to make more sense.

Autistic Trait: Copying your tone of voice or accent.

Common Misinterpretation(s): Trying to get attention, trying to be dramatic, being rude, and/or disrespecting authority.

What's Really Happening:

When I was a child, I picked up accents, tones of voice, intonation, speech patterns, etc., from TV shows and movies I watched. As soon as I was done watching a movie, I would talk like the characters wherever I went, sometimes quoting lines outright.

Of course, I know now that it was a combination of echolalia and scripting, but back then, people just thought it was yet another thing I was doing for attention – or to be rude or to disrespect authority, etc. The thing is, after I watched TV or a movie, I knew I was copying the accents, but when I talked to someone with a different accent or a marked difference in the way they spoke, I would "catch" the way they spoke and mimic it without having any idea I was doing it.

Just like in other cases of things I did that people found off-putting, people would become suddenly offended, but since they didn't directly say, *"You're copying my accent"* or *"You're making fun of the way I speak"*, I couldn't connect my behavior to their response.

Honestly, even if they did say that directly, I was already so self-protective at a young age and thought everyone around me just randomly made things up to yell at me for no reason, I probably still wouldn't have believed it because I couldn't hear that I was doing it.

If your autistic loved one "catches" accents, they're likely not doing it to make fun of anyone, and there's no hidden social agenda. It's probably just a combination of echolalia, scripting, and masking.

Autistic Trait: Being uncomfortable when eating around others.

Common Misinterpretation(s): Being overly picky, controlling, and manipulative, being rude, disrespecting authority, and/or thinking we are better than others.

What's Really Happening:

Some autistic people experience misophonia, a hypersensitivity to certain sounds that triggers the fight-or-flight response as well as feelings of aggression and rage. Those with misophonia may often find eating with others to be intolerable due to the sounds of chewing, swallowing, and utensils clicking against teeth. I, personally, cannot stand the sound of swallowing due to my own misophonia.

This is what the sound of swallowing is like for me:

Imagine somebody put noise-canceling headphones on your ears, turned the dial to 10, added some echo and reverb, and then piped the sound of someone eating the biggest, juiciest apple to ever fall from a tree while washing it down with an ice-cold glass of full fat milk. As the person eats, you hear each individual piece of mashed fruit and every drop of dairy product squish together into a thick, unholy glob of mash that slowly slides its way down their throat in one booming, epiglottal gulp – and then they take another bite. This horror continues for 20 minutes.

I cannot eat in the same room with someone else unless the TV is on. Every single swallow sends me into an involuntary spasm and makes me feel like my nerves are on fire. If the autistic person in your life has a similar sensory profile, they're not avoiding you, they're avoiding triggering sounds that send them into fight or flight. Another reason your autistic loved one may not feel comfortable eating with others is they may only be able to tolerate certain foods due to sensory sensitivities, and their eating habits have been previously scrutinized.

Autistic Trait: Significant distress at changed plans.

Common Misinterpretation(s): Trying to be dramatic, being ungrateful, being selfish, being overly controlling or manipulative, being rude, trying to cause conflict or drama, not caring about others, and/or thinking we are better than others.

What's Really Happening:

Change can be very difficult for autistic people to cope with, and it can cause significant distress, meltdowns, and/or shutdowns because our brains process and navigate the world differently from neurotypicals.

In an earlier section, I gave an example of a teenager coming home from school to find a surprise birthday party waiting for her. Her literal, linear brain and stressed-out body could not cope with the unexpected sensory information and social expectations. Furthermore, she felt 'stuck' because the sudden social obligation forced her to abandon her routine.

Here's a visual representation of why this is so stressful: Imagine your routine is a freshly printed manuscript sitting on a desk by an open window. All the pages are in the correct order, and when you sit down to read, the story is cohesive. Now, imagine a gust of wind comes in and blows the papers around and out of order. If you tried to read it then, the story would make no sense.

The change is the gust of wind, and routine is the manuscript that got blown around. The distress, shutdown, or meltdown is the act of painstakingly gathering each page, dusting it off, and putting the whole thing back together again to form a cohesive story. Since neurotypical brains are more like bound books, a gust of wind (a change in routine) won't affect them nearly as much, but for a loose manuscript, a gust of wind (a change in routine) can blow everything out of order (and cause a great deal of energy to fix).

Autistic Trait: Not audibly saying 'thank you' (for speaking individuals).

Common Misinterpretation(s): Being ungrateful, being selfish, being manipulative, not caring about others, and/or thinking we are better than others.

What's Really Happening:

This may not be a common one, but I've struggled with it my whole life, so it's possible your autistic loved one may struggle with it, as well. This kind of ties into not responding the way neurotypical people expect when receiving a gift, but it also extends to favors done, trips planned, help given, events attended, etc.

When someone does any of these things for me, I feel immense gratitude. I feel like it shines from my heart into my eyes and beams from my face in cascading waves of tender appreciation that the other person can clearly see and feel. But no. They just see my usual blank facial expression that I still, occasionally, forget I have to manually animate.

I have always had such difficulty saying the words, "thank you" because I truly don't remember them. It's similar to how everything is out of sight, out of mind and how I forget faces and names. And I may really have strong emotions, but for some reason, those emotions don't funnel down into those two words that are so strongly expected in neurotypical society.

My gratitude always feels like it requires more of a response than a simple, "thank you", which is probably another reason I don't remember to say it. It doesn't feel natural, it doesn't feel organic. It actually feels fake, lacking, not enough of a response to someone's kindness.

If your autistic loved one never says these words or expresses their gratitude verbally (even if they are a speaking person), this doesn't mean that they don't feel gratitude and aren't showing it in ways you may not readily pick up on. It's not meant as a purposeful slight against you.

Autistic Trait: Not responding to requests expressed as statements.

Common Misinterpretation(s): Being selfish, not caring about others, being cold and calculated, disrespecting authority, and/or being lazy and unmotivated.

What's Really Happening:

"The kitchen needs to be cleaned." "It's cold in here." "This bill needs to be paid." "There's poop on the floor."

There's a story behind that last one. One time, when I was living at my aunt's house, I came home, and she told me one of the dogs had pooped on the floor. I looked down and sidestepped the mess. Yep. One of the dogs had, indeed, pooped on the floor. I continued to avoid it as I took groceries inside, and my aunt continued to tell me about it. Once I put the groceries away and sat down, she sighed, got up, cleaned up the poop and sat back down. *"Why didn't you clean up the poop?"*

"Huh?! "You didn't ask me to!?"

Now, that was not me being a sarcastic jerk. I wasn't trying to snarkily say that since she didn't ask me to do it specifically, I purposefully didn't do it just to be mean. No. What I meant was, I had no idea she wanted me to pick it up or do anything about it because **my brain literally doesn't translate statements as requests**. I thought she was just warning me not to step in it. If she'd asked me to pick it up, I would have done it with no problem.

The same goes for the other statements listed above. Neurotypical brains usually translate them as someone indirectly communicating their needs while the autistic brain translates them into literal statements. We usually take words at face value. If you need or want something from your autistic loved one, ask them directly. Be explicit. Don't hint. It only sets them up for failure.

Autistic Trait: Not greeting neighbors, classmates, co-workers, etc., upon seeing them.

Common Misinterpretation(s): Being selfish, being rude, and/or thinking we are better than others.

What's Really Happening:

I remember reading a story posted on a forum by an autistic woman who was about 50 years old. She lived alone in an apartment complex with her dog, and she would often take the dog out for walks. If she happened to pass a neighbor in the hall, in the elevator, or on the street, she never greeted them. She rarely even looked at them.

When apartment management pointed out that the other tenants thought she was rude, she was shocked. She didn't understand how they could think she was rude when they didn't even know her, but that was the issue for them, *the fact that she never greeted them!*

This woman had no idea that there was a hidden social expectation to greet her neighbors. I was the same way for a long time, too. It would never have occurred to me to just say, *"Hi"* to someone as I passed them in the hall, the store, at work, or in class. Conversations, for me, were limited to relevant topics, not just saying 'hello' or small talk. I didn't understand the purpose of it, and I didn't even know it was expected of me.

I've had people ask, *"How could you not know that?"* about this and other "obvious" neurotypical social expectations. I have no idea how to explain how I don't know something. I just didn't. This may be the case with the autistic person in your life, too.

It saddens me to know that so many autistic, shy, introverted, etc., people are automatically seen as rude just because they don't greet others. It can cause an innocent person to develop a reputation and be mistreated for something they aren't even aware of, which can cause trauma.

Autistic Trait: Not having "common sense".

Common Misinterpretation(s): Everything in the *The Confusing and Traumatic Accusations We Receive Everyday* section of this book.

What's Really Happening:

I'm going to go out on a limb here and say that common sense is a myth. It doesn't exist. While there are certain communities (schools, neighborhoods, towns) where people have shared experiences that give them similar knowledge and thought processes that are "common" within that particular group, this does not mean that anyone outside that group is privy to this same knowledge.

There are varying reasons for this, but neurodivergence is a big one. Since many autistic people are bottom-up thinkers and explicit learners (instead of top-down thinkers and implicit learners like neurotypical people), we don't often "pick up" on the information neurotypical people seem to automatically absorb from simply being in an environment.

Autistic people learn best when given lots of details and are taught in a specific, deliberate manner with clear and concise language and step-based instruction.

You may question why the autistic person in your life can't do something **they've seen you do** dozens of times or doesn't seem to know something you've **talked about around them** for years, but that's because their brains don't function that way. Remember, not only are our sensory systems heightened, we also have to manually filter out all of the sensory information in our environment while masking our traits while simultaneously processing the world with a brain that is already jam-packed full of ideas, thoughts, song lyrics, memories, to-do lists, feelings, etc. swirling throughout our brains in technicolor every moment of the day.

To learn, we have to free up some space on the hard drive!

Autistic Trait: Taking you literally when you invite them out.

Common Misinterpretation(s): Being selfish, making everything about us, being controlling or manipulative, trying to steal someone's romantic partner, trying to cause conflict or drama, and/or not caring about others.

What's Really Happening:

By default, the autistic brain processes language literally. It's only through painful and embarrassing trial and error that we eventually realize we live in a world where the predominant neurotype often does not say what they mean and mean what they say. Instead, they rely on a complex set of seemingly contradictory words, gestures, facial expressions, vocal tone, and innuendo to get their needs, wants, and feelings across to each other.

Imagine our shock when people seem constantly annoyed with us because they perceive us as ignoring them, being sarcastic, trying to start arguments, etc., when **we're simply responding literally to the words** without seeing the non-verbal communication that sometimes directly contradicts those words!

Many autistic people, when we first enter the more complex social world of adulthood, have no idea that when someone says, *"We should go get coffee sometime and catch up"* that it's just a social nicety, a way to end the conversation on a polite note, or both, but not an actual invitation. It's not meant to be taken literally, but we don't know that until we've mortified ourselves by following up about that "coffee date" until the neurotypical person tells us off and blocks us! It's even worse when a couple is hanging out, and they run into their autistic friend. *"Hey, you want to join us for the movie?"* The autistic friend takes the invite literally and joins them, then wonders why they're getting dirty looks all night.

Don't invite autistic people out if you don't literally mean it. It's confusing, and it sets us up for social failure.

Autistic Trait: Being honest when you ask for their honest opinion.

Common Misinterpretation(s): Being rude or aggressive.

What's Really Happening:

"What do you think of this dress? You can be honest!" If you say that to a neurotypical person, they will still know that you secretly want them to tell you what you want to hear. If you ask an autistic person this, you're going to get their 100% honest opinion. So, if they hate it, they'll tell you.

If you then get offended and yell at them for being honest, which you just told them it was safe to do, you've led them into a social trap, and now you're gaslighting them. Even if that's not your intention, you're still causing psychological harm.

As people who take words at face value, living through a lifetime of people telling us it's "OK" to be honest when it's actually some sort of social test or trap we don't understand, has done serious damage. It's never OK to do this to someone, especially when you know good and well that the person thinks and processes the world differently from you. When their honesty is actually an asset that makes them a trustworthy person in the world, you violate that trust when you set your autistic friend up in this way. Please don't do it.

Your autistic friend is not rude, aggressive, or "too much" when they give you an honest answer to your question, especially when you've insisted on honesty, when you've given them a verbal indicator that total honesty is what's wanted in that particular situation. When I hear stories about stuff like this happening, I imagine a young deer being coaxed lovingly into a trap by a hunter who intends to kill it. It feels sinister to me, purposeful, planned.

If you've ever wondered why so many autistic people struggle to trust the majority of neurotypical people, and why we are so traumatized – this is why.

Autistic Trait: Not wanting to spend time with family.

Common Misinterpretation(s): Hiding something, being ungrateful, being selfish, being rude, secretly hating everyone, playing victim, and/or holding grudges.

What's Really Happening:

People who have healthy, close bonds with their family members often see those estranged from their family as bad people. After all, how could anyone not want to spend time with people who make you feel so safe, comfortable, and understood? How could you not want to catch up, have fun, and exchange stories?

That's easy. Not everyone's experience of family is like this.

It always amazes me that healthy, well-adjusted people look down on those who choose to avoid their families because they're looking at this decision through their own clear, untraumatized lenses. *They* equate family time with happiness and connection, so anyone who *doesn't* want happiness and connection must be a bad person, right?

What if that estranged person's experience of family has actually been anything but love, acceptance, fun, and compassion? What if the reason they avoid them is because they are, in fact, truly good and trustworthy people who, if they spent time with family, they'd be forced to be around people who weren't?

For autistic people, time with family can mean having to deal with constant disbelief about neurology, members being angry and offended during the visit, frequent boundary violations, and bullying. Not to mention sensory overload, routine disruption, forced masking, and social exhaustion.

Not everyone can safely be around their relatives, and that's OK.

Autistic Trait: Appearing to ignore you when you're stern or angry.

Common Misinterpretation(s): Hiding something, trying to be dramatic, being controlling, being bored or disinterested, being rude, disrespecting authority, playing victim, and/or feeling sorry for ourselves.

What's Really Happening:

Many autistic people, especially those who were late diagnosed, like myself, have complex post-traumatic stress disorder. Since many of us have had experiences where we've been yelled at, reprimanded, and even physically harmed seemingly "out of nowhere", we may have unexpected reactions to anyone showing frustration or anger or having a stern tone around us.

Some autistic people who have been traumatized will smile or laugh when being told off, accused of something, or yelled at. It's not disrespect, and it's not an indicator that we've purposefully done whatever we're being accused of. It's a stress response.

Other autistic people who have experienced lifelong trauma will appear to "go blank" when someone raises their voice. Their eyes will glaze over, their jaw will go slack, they'll answer in more of a monotone voice than you're used to. They may suddenly start agreeing with whatever you say even if they haven't done what you're accusing them of. This is called fawning, and it is a trauma response.

Many people know about the fight-or-flight response, but you may not be aware of freezing and fawning. Freezing is when the body and brain shuts down in response to a perceived threat, and fawning is when a person tries to appease the person they feel threatened by, thereby disarming them, soothing their anger, and protecting themselves from danger.

Do not raise your voice to a traumatized autistic person. Regulate your emotions first before confronting them about anything.

Autistic Trait: Not being able to find things (even in "plain sight").

Common Misinterpretation(s): Trying to get attention, trying to be dramatic, being cold and calculated, playing innocent, playing victim, being lazy and unmotivated, and making excuses.

What's Really Happening:

Have you ever asked your autistic loved one to get something for you from the next room, and they've come back empty-handed and looking a bit panicked? This isn't something they're doing on purpose to be lazy or prank you or get out of doing something. It's because they genuinely cannot find what it is you're asking them to find.

Personally, I've always had this problem. If you ask me to pick an individual object off a desk or in a cabinet, I'll have a very, very difficult time locating that object because my brain turns multiple objects on the same surface into what I have coined 'The Amorphous Blob of OneThing'. My brain can't seem to separate large masses of objects into individual objects right away. It takes time for me to sort through what I'm seeing and locate the specific item I'm looking for.

When I was a child, in addition to not being able to find the object, I would hear frustrated sighs and questions about what was taking so long, so I would panic as seconds ticked by, and my frantic eyes still didn't fall on the requested object. I eventually gave up, cried, and walked back out to the area where they were and told them, with all honesty, that I couldn't find it. Of course, the person would get up in a huff, stroll to the next room, find the object immediately, come back out, and wave it around while accusing me of pretending.

I was never pretending. I just needed more time, patience from others, and detail about exactly where in the pile it was supposedly located. Also, being told color, size, and approximate shape helps tremendously.

Autistic Trait: Consistently speaking at a high volume.

Common Misinterpretation(s): Trying to get attention, being controlling, manipulative, aggressive, rude, and/or disrespecting authority.

What's Really Happening:

I've always struggled with speaking at a high volume. When I was a child, people thought I was doing it for attention (they thought a lot of my natural autistic traits were because I wanted attention), but I actually do not like attention; I do not like to be perceived except for in situations that I closely monitor and control.

Before I learned to mask, my speech was loud, and my vocal tone was flat, so I would just go around yelling in long, rambling, monotone monologues thinking I was having a conversation and not understanding why people were doing everything they could to get away from me.

The thing is, I couldn't hear it. I didn't hear how loud my voice was or how flat it was, and I couldn't tell that I was monologuing. I didn't know how give-and-take conversation worked because it was not something that came naturally to me.

In the case of your autistic loved one, they may not hear that they're talking way above the volume they need to be heard. Also, they may also speak louder because of their own inability to filter out background noise. Since many autistic people hear everything at equal (and sometimes deafening) volume, we may "shout" over background noise, so you can hear us, not realizing that you barely hear the background noise because your neurotypical brain automatically filters it out for you!

If your autistic loved one speaks loudly, please don't speak loudly back or yell at them to try to "show them how they sound". That just feels like an attack that came from nowhere. Calmly explain their vocal volume and come up with a silent indicator you can use in public situations.

Autistic Trait: Appearing to ignore household chores and responsibilities.

Common Misinterpretation(s): Being selfish, not caring about others, being lazy and unmotivated, and/or making excuses.

What's Really Happening:

If the autistic person in your life also has ADHD and/or poor working memory (like I do), they may struggle mightily with household chores and responsibilities that you, as a neurotypical person, find easy to remember and get done.

I've seen parents say that their autistic/ADHD child "ignores" their chore list, and it always rubs me the wrong way because not only is it an unfair accusation, but it also doesn't make any logical sense. It would be more accurate to say that the autistic person **does not remember** their chore list, or they **don't see** what needs to be done without specific instruction. Another empowering way to see this is, their chore list/expectations are currently **inaccessible** to them. (This way, the blame doesn't fall solely on the autistic person's shoulders.)

The act of ignoring is *purposeful*. Ignoring means you see something, and you willfully choose to pay it no mind. Therefore, accusing an autistic or ADHD person of *ignoring* their chore list is illogical because the reason behind the chores not getting done is *not* a purposeful act but a difference in brain function. One describes *conscious will and purposeful intent* (ignoring), the other (doesn't remember) is a result of brain wiring. Instead of spending your energy lecturing after the fact, work with your autistic loved one to make chore lists and expectations accessible by supplying clear, concise instructions and visual aids, and taking advantage of reminder apps. Keep in mind that scolding someone with a poor memory for forgetting to do a chore is just as unfair and traumatic as punishing someone who needs glasses for not being able to see without them.

Autistic Trait: Appears to ignore you when you're speaking or non-verbally expressing an emotion or social need.

Common Misinterpretation(s): Being bored or disinterested, being rude, trying to cause conflict or drama, not caring about others, being cold and calculated, disrespecting authority, secretly hating others, holding grudges, and thinking we are better than others.

What's Really Happening:

Autistic people are accused of ignoring a lot, which is why I'm bringing it up as its own separate topic here. We don't only get accused of purposefully ignoring what needs to be done in a household or at a job (when, in reality, our neurodivergent brains just need specific instructions and clearly laid-out expectations), we are also told we ignore others when they speak to us or when they non-verbally express an emotion or a social need.

Again, it's the word "ignore" that bothers me because it's inaccurate and misleading. Ignoring is a purposeful and conscious act, but being unaware, not remembering, not hearing, or not understanding is not. It goes back to the glasses example for me.

If you waved at your neighbor sitting on their front porch as they walked by, but they did not wave back, you may ask your neighbor about it the next day. An explanation of, *"Oh, I'm sorry. I wasn't wearing my glasses!"* will feel entirely different for you than, *"Yeah, I saw you. I just don't particularly like you."* You likely wouldn't even be upset anymore once the neighbor explained he'd forgotten to wear his glasses, but if he outright told you he ignored you on purpose, you'd be insulted!

It's the same concept here. An autistic person who appears to ignore you may; 1) Be unaware of your non-verbal cues, 2) Take your questions at face value and answer them literally without elaborating as you may expect, or 3) Be hyper-focused and not hear your greeting even if you're right next to them.

Autistic Trait: Interrupts to ask for details when you're telling a story.

Common Misinterpretation(s): One-upping others, being selfish, making everything about us, being controlling, and/or not caring about others.

What's Really Happening:

Autistic interrupting is often as deeply misinterpreted and gets as strong a negative emotional reaction as autistic ignoring, which is why I think it's critical to explain what's happening from our perspective.

Details are incredibly important to the autistic brain because it helps us not only fully understand your story, but it also helps us to empathize in a deeper, more genuine way.

This is why, when you're telling a story, instead of nodding politely and gently prompting all the way through (the way most neurotypical people do and expect), autistic folks will frequently stop you and ask for details because, to us, it shows interest and a desire to fully immerse ourselves in your experience.

It also helps us form a complete picture of what you're going through while simultaneously clearing up any inconsistencies that may be present in the story, so our brains don't snag on one confusing detail and miss everything else.

Let me explain that part a bit better: When you tell a story that leads with emotion, you may have a few logical inconsistencies that a neurotypical listener's brain will automatically correct but the autistic brain will snag on, drawing our attention away from what's important; your experience.

Moreover, the autistic person in your life may also have a poor memory and be unable to hold questions until the end. **Hint:** Let them write them down. It's not encouraging impolite behavior, it's providing accessibility.

Autistic Trait: Laughing at your angry facial expressions.

Common Misinterpretation(s): Hiding something, being rude, trying to cause conflict or drama, not caring about others, and/or disrespecting authority.

What's Really Happening:

This may not be a common one, but I wanted to include it because I've seen others mention it, and it's definitely something I've struggled with.

For some reason, my brain registers certain angry facial expressions as hilariously funny, and that's ironic because anger terrifies me. I don't like yelling or conflict or sudden, loud noises, but my brain reads certain types of angry facial expressions so incorrectly, I react as though I'm watching a sitcom. A jutting chin, bulging eyes, flared nostrils, bared teeth, pursed lips, deep frowns, all of those, especially any of them put together seem cartoonish, like a caricature of anger instead of real anger, and my first instinct is to laugh.

Maybe it's because I don't express anger this way. I get quiet, I go still as a statue, my muscles tense, my eyelids get heavy and start to close into slits, my lips and nostrils twitch, and I feel like I'm vibrating all over with a hum of dangerous energy. However, most neurotypical people don't read me as angry during those times, just quiet and sullen at most. They don't laugh, but they don't register me as angry, either, so it looks like the misunderstanding may go both ways.

Even certain non-exaggerated angry facial expressions confuse me. Even though I don't laugh at those, I don't always read them as anger. For example, knitted brows and squinted eyes read as confusion to me because that's how I express confusion.

If you're angry with the autistic person in your life, tell them in plain words.

Autistic Trait: Appear to be making excuses for their behavior.

Common Misinterpretation(s): Hiding something, having a hidden agenda, having an angle, being controlling, manipulative, aggressive, or rude, not caring about others, and/or disrespecting authority.

What's Really Happening:

This one caused traumatic, unending circular conversations with others that I found confusing, exhausting, and ultimately so psychologically damaging, I think it's one of the primary reasons I have complex PTSD. From my point of view, I was being purposefully and mercilessly gaslit when, in reality, it was a massive difference in perception and communication. For many neurotypical people, being given a logical explanation after they were offended by another reads as an attempt to dodge accountability while also avoiding showing empathy. A logical explanation also sounds like an attempt to downplay the other person's feelings or even gaslight *them* into doubting their own perception.

For the autistic person, however, a logical explanation *is* a show of empathy, and I'll explain why. If someone tells me I've hurt their feelings, my immediate thought is, *"Oh, my God! This person thinks I've hurt them on purpose. Let me quickly explain what I actually meant, so their feelings aren't hurt anymore, and they feel safe around me again."*

Apologizing doesn't occur to me because the offense wasn't purposeful, and since having things explained to me significantly reduces *my* feelings of being hurt, it's hard for me to understand that it doesn't work that way for neurotypical people. I've never understood why people hurt others for a laugh, to get ahead socially, or because they're "evening the score" on someone who hurt them long ago. I just don't operate like that. The only time I hurt other people is either by accident or in self-defense, and in the case of self-defense, the situation has to be pretty extreme because my automatic response is to remove myself from the situation – not harm others.

Autistic Trait: Revealing your personal details or secrets to others.

Common Misinterpretation(s): Being manipulative and/or rude, trying to start conflict or drama, not caring about others, being cold and calculated, and/or holding grudges.

What's Really Happening:

If the autistic person in your life has revealed a personal detail or secret about you that you thought was just between you and your loved one, it doesn't mean they did it with malicious intent.

Since many autistic people don't have an automatic, ingrained sense of social hierarchy as it applies to neurotypical society, and we tend to be much more open, honest, and vocal about our everyday experiences, the things that neurotypical people view as secrets may not be to us.

One of my most embarrassing moments in childhood was my mother telling me, in detail, what she thought of the family of a friend of mine, and me, having been taught that "honesty is the best policy", answered truthfully when my friend asked me what she'd thought the next time I saw her after my first sleepover at her house.

I eagerly told her that my mom said her house smelled bad, it looked like nobody bathed, and one of their older male family members looked like he creeped on kids. I know – painfully cringeworthy. It was 30 years ago, and I still wince when I think about it, but she was my best friend, and I thought best friends told each other everything! (My naivete knew *NO* bounds!) If you're wondering, yes, my mom is autistic, too. lol!

So, yeah. If something is a secret, *please explicitly tell your autistic loved one that*, and don't expect them to just know, even if it seems like "common sense" to you.

Autistic Trait: Appearing to only call or reach out when they need something.

Common Misinterpretation(s): Having a hidden agenda, having an angle, being ungrateful, being selfish, rude, and/or cold and calculated.

What's Really Happening:

I don't like phone calls. I haven't liked them since I was a teenager, and they were my only option. I actually have my voicemail set up to let people know that I don't remember to check my voicemail and to please text me or email me, and then I give them the email address. It may sound rude to some, but I want to normalize speaking up for one's neurodivergent needs. I think it's important if we are to create a more neuroinclusive world.

That said, there are times when I will exclusively communicate by telephone, and that's in emergencies and moments of emotional crisis. If I'm sobbing, all bets are off, I'm calling you. I mean, I'm already upset, so making a call won't make things worse as far as sensory issues or auditory processing challenges. It literally never occurs to me to pick up the phone and call someone just to chat. My autistic brain never could make sense of that because it sees no point in small talk and catching up on mundane, everyday life experiences.

For me, communication has to have a reason, there has to be a pre-determined and meaningful topic. When I was diagnosed with breast cancer in 2020, I had no problem talking to people on the phone that I wouldn't ordinarily be able to talk because there was an understood topic of conversation, and I knew nobody would take that opportunity to dredge up things from my past or ask me unanswerable questions like, *"Why don't you ever call us?"* Neurotypical decorum for the win there!

If your autistic loved one reaches out only when there's an emergency or big news, they likely have a similar view of the purpose of communication.

Autistic Trait: Needing to talk things out and achieve closure, even after a minor misunderstanding or falling out.

Common Misinterpretation(s): Trying to be dramatic, being controlling and manipulative, trying to cause conflict or drama, playing victim, and/or holding grudges.

What's Really Happening:

I made two separate posts about closure and needing to talk things out on my Instagram page because I feel like they are separate issues, but I also feel like they go hand-in-hand, so I combined them here.

Some readers, as is inevitable when you're posting on social media, made comments like, *"Doesn't everyone need closure and to talk things out? That's not an exclusively autistic thing."*

OK, yes, but actually, no. Because here's the thing: If all people of all neurotypes needed to talk things out for hours, sometimes days, and make sure that every little detail is explained, analyzed, and cataloged, and that every single feeling and misunderstanding and point of view is whittled down to its marrow, then us autistic folks wouldn't hear things like, *"Get over it, already!"* or *"Move on!"*, or *"Are you still on that?"* or *"Why can't you ever let things go?"* Neurotypical and autistic people both experience similar things a lot of the time, but for autistic people, it is often at triple the severity. It's the same for the need for closure.

After experiences of deep emotional upheaval, both neurotypical and autistic people need closure. However, an autistic person may need to talk about a minor disagreement for hours or days just to feel emotionally safe with someone again, and we often find it impossible to just "let go" of something without balancing that equation first. This can come across as "harping" on a topic, but it's essential for our emotional well-being to process every detail in full.

How to Communicate Your Feelings Without Causing a Trauma Response

OK, so now that you know all this; now that you understand that your autistic loved one is not purposefully offending and insulting you on a daily basis, and that they just communicate differently from you, how do you express how your neurotypical brain experiences these communication differences if you *do* find them insulting or hurtful?

I have a formula for that, and it can work much more effectively than how you may be communicating your feelings now because this formula is more accessible to the autistic brain.

It's important to keep in mind that the reason you may get a defensive response from the autistic person in your life when you communicate your feelings is because *the way you communicate is just as foreign and confusing to us as the way we communicate is to you.*

When you lead with an emotionally charged response to something your autistic loved one has said or done that you find hurtful, it's as jarring and unexpected to us as it would be if someone you were having a pleasant conversation with suddenly blasted an air horn in your face.

It doesn't make sense to us, it scrambles our senses, it causes us to go into fight-or-flight. We can't focus on processing how you feel or trying to apologize to you because, for us, **your reaction is coming out of absolutely nowhere**.

Your neurotypical brain translates what your autistic loved one has said into a purposeful insult, and you respond to that insult the way you would respond to anyone offending you on purpose.

Meanwhile, your autistic loved one, who was communicating according to their natural brain wiring by stating a fact, revealing a secret, missing a social cue, etc., with no malicious intent whatsoever, suddenly finds themselves being yelled at in the middle of what they believed to be a perfectly pleasant and non-threatening conversation.

Instead of shocking your autistic loved one's nervous system into fight-or-flight, shutdown, or meltdown, try communicating your feelings using this formula:

1. Regulate your own emotions first.

The very first step you need to take when you feel offended by anything the autistic person has said or done is to regulate your own emotions first.

Many autistic people are traumatized due to a lifetime of being suddenly yelled at for seemingly no reason. Because of this, many of us have very, very heightened nervous systems (even beyond the heightened nervous systems we would have for simply being autistic).

This means that even if your mood shifts ever-so-slightly, even if the energy in the room shifts by a hair, a traumatized autistic person's brain and nervous system will already start going into fight-or-flight before the person is fully conscious that this is even happening.

This built-in threat detection system is usually the first thing you'll bump up against when communicating a perceived offense to an autistic person with post-traumatic stress.

If your emotions aren't regulated, you've already lost. It's not that your loved one is trying to shut you out or that they don't care about your feelings, it's that you cannot effectively communicate with someone in fight-or-flight, and your loved one cannot stop the process once it starts.

It's an automatic self-preservation mechanism your autistic loved one's nervous system put into place to survive in a world where sudden yelling could come from anyone at any time.

2. Be sure you have the autistic person's full, undivided attention.

If you feel offended by something the autistic person in your life said or did a few hours or days ago, this step will especially apply. Although, it may still apply even if the perceived offense happened a minute ago because, for us autistic/ADHD-combined types, we may be three topics ahead and/or moved on to the next project before you've even had a chance to fully process the word or deed you found offensive.

Before any conversation happens, always be sure you have your autistic loved one's full, undivided attention. If they're involved in a project of their intense interest, exhausted from the day, dysregulated from the environment, or have anything else going on that's taking up the bulk of their attention and energy, they may not remember or understand what you're trying to convey.

Be sure your autistic loved one is fully aware, regulated, and present before having this type of discussion.

3. Tell them what they did or said.

This one is so critical, and it gets skipped over a lot because the assumption is that the autistic person is aware of what they said or did, especially if the incident just occurred, even if they aren't aware it came across as offensive.

This isn't always true. It's not that your autistic loved one doesn't remember what happened (although, depending on the person's memory and attention span as well as how long ago the incident occurred, that may be the case), it's that the *intention* behind the words or actions, not the words or actions themselves, that will most likely be at the forefront of their minds.

Instead, report the specific incident to them like a news outlet. Just the facts. *"At this time, during this moment, you said or did the following."*

4. Tell them how what they did or said affected you.

After you've given the facts and stated what was said or done and when it was said or done, tell them how it affected you emotionally. Be descriptive but avoid accusations. Use "I" statements. Instead of, *"You made me feel this way"*, say, *"I felt [insert emotion] when you [insert word or action]."*

5. Tell them why it is considered socially inappropriate to do or say that (or why it triggered a trauma response for you).

When you get to this step, it's critical to remember that the way an autistic person relates to others is different than the way a neurotypical person relates to others, and neither are wrong.

Be sure to keep this in mind when explaining why any neurotypical person might be offended by what they said or did (or why you, personally, find what they said or did offensive).

Something like, *"When neurotypical people do or say [x], it is generally seen as [x] because it usually means [x] when neurotypical people do or say it."*

6. Allow them to ask clarifying questions and to explain their intent and perspective.

Immediately following an explanation of how a neurotypical person might view what was said or done, your autistic loved one may be truly shocked (because, again, we socialize and relate differently than you) and have lots of follow-up questions and also feel the need to explain what their actual intent was (which is fair considering you just explained how what was said or done is viewed from a neurotypical perspective).

Please do not discourage this.

When your autistic loved one explains their intentions, it's not to invalidate your feelings or make excuses, it's a show of empathy. It is an attempt to repair a rupture in your relationship while restoring a sense of safety and emotional balance.

When they ask follow-up questions, it's not an attempt to overpower you, it's a way to get a deeper understanding of your feelings and point of view, so the same problems don't occur in the future.

7. Tell them what you need them to do instead.

Communicate your needs clearly and concisely, so your autistic loved one knows exactly what you need and expect from them in the future.

Communication and Understanding Needs to Be a Two-Way Street

While that formula can help significantly reduce the number of difficult interactions between you and your autistic loved one, it's very important to remember that communication needs to be a two-way street.

What I mean is, there are going to be plenty of things that you, as a neurotypical person, naturally say and do with no ill intentions that will be hurtful and offensive to the autistic person in your life.

This is why they need to be able to use the formula with you (or one that works for them). They need to have just as much agency and the right to communicate their feelings and needs to you as you do with them.

You will both need to be able to compromise because, for too long, neurotypical people have had all the power and say in what is considered socially acceptable for everyone.

This has led to the creation and implementation of emotionally manipulative and deeply traumatizing training regimes disguised as therapy in an attempt to force autistic people into conforming to standards their brains and bodies were never meant to conform to.

Instead, what we should be doing is focusing on teaching the ways and merits of *both* communication types, so we can all learn, grow, and advance as one unified human race.

The Takeaway

I'm not sure if I can do a TL;DR (too long, didn't read) version of this book, but I can tell you this; one of the best things you can do right now for your autistic loved one is to believe them. Believe them when they tell you it's too loud, too bright, and too confusing. Believe them when they tell you they don't know why you're angry, and that your anger is scaring them. Believe them when they tell you that they need you to explain what's upsetting you, even if you think it's plain as day.

They're not being dramatic, they're not looking for attention or a way out of accountability; *their brains simply do not work the way yours does* (if you are a non-autistic person). Believe and trust in that if nothing else for now. Go through the book again when you have the time and bandwidth, make notes in the margins, go over the material directly with your autistic loved one, ask for feedback.

As I said in the beginning of this book, it's meant to be a guide. It won't describe every autistic person, but some of the traits that are frequently misinterpreted will resonate, and that's a great place to start and get the conversation going!

If you need more help or you have questions, I offer private consultations I call 'translation sessions' that you can book with me for personalized advice and recommendations. I'd be happy to help.

Visit: www.thearticulateautistic.com and click on 'Private Consultations for Autistic People & Their Loved Ones' to book a free, 15-minute call to get to know each other and see if we'd be a good fit to work together.

I hope you found this guide helpful, and I look forward to hearing from you.

Jaime

Printed in Great Britain
by Amazon

41912913R00044